LIVE AND LEARN AND PASS IT ON

People ages 5 to 95 share what they've discovered
about life, love, and other good stuff.

Written and compiled by H. Jackson Brown, Jr.

RUTLEDGE HILL PRESS
Nashville, Tennessee

Published in Nashville, Tennessee, by Rutledge Hill Press, Inc., 513 Third Avenue South, Nashville, Tennessee 37210. Distributed in Canada by H. B. Fenn and Company Ltd., Mississauga, Ontario.

Typography by D&T/Bailey Typesetting, Inc., Nashville, Tennessee

Library of Congress Cataloging-in-Publication Data

Live and learn and pass it on: people ages 5 to 95 share what they've learned about life, love, and other good stuff/written and compiled by H. Jackson Brown, Jr.
    p. cm.
  ISBN 1-55853-156-4
  1. Life cycle, Human — Miscellanea. 2. Developmental psychology — Miscellanea. 3. Maturation (Psychology) — Miscellanea. I. Brown. H. Jackson, 1940–
HQ799.95.L55   1991   91-32132
158'.1 — dc20   CIP

Printed in the United States of America
5 6 7 8 9 10 11 12 13 — 93 92

INTRODUCTION

ON THE morning of my fifty-first birthday, I thought it would be interesting to jot down a few things more than half a century of living had taught me.

I wrote, "I've learned that..." twenty times on the left-hand side of a piece of lined notebook paper and proceeded to complete the twenty sentences.

It was such an enjoyable exercise that I decided to add to it every Sunday morning. I soon had quite a list. I mentioned it to a friend at lunch, and he said he would like to create his own list. Other friends and acquaintances joined the project.

To broaden the age group, I enlisted the help of kindergarten kids, seventh and eighth graders, high school students, young married couples, and senior citizens. Eventually hundreds of people of all ages and backgrounds participated.

Editing their entries convinced me that wisdom knows no age and "truth is truth no matter where you find it."

This book contains the combined wisdom and learning experiences of thousands of years of living. It is what we have been taught by our parents, spouses, children, pastors, teachers, friends, and enemies. It is lessons learned from loving and winning and loving and losing, from the school of hard knocks, and the old method of trial and error.

I was surprised and delighted that several people ended their lists with the statement, "I've learned that I still have a lot to learn." As, indeed, we all do.

Regardless of how much we know, it is never enough. But that's OK because every day, with every new experience, we are offered new opportunities for discovery and growth.

School is always in session and life challenges us to excel at being both enthusiastic student and inspired teacher.

H. J. B.
Tall Pine Lodge
Fernvale, Tennessee
February 1, 1992

Acknowledgments

MY GRATEFUL THANKS to all who contributed to this collection of discoveries and insights: Rosemary Brown, Adam Brown, Sallie Bett Crowell, Wade Watson, Shannon Stinson, Lori DeSanders, Emily Merriwether, Marian Meyerson, David Redford, Gifford Vance, Lee Wilson, Morris MacKenzie, Steven Curtiswood, Marnie Salyer, Franklin Powers, Oscar Liebman, Irene Copeland, Rusty Brakefield, Allan Rhodes, David and Jeanne Siefert, Marguerite Grady, Col. Henry Cullum, Warner Brooks, Patti Comini, Tony Gonzales, Houston Samuelson, Ann Wagner, Lenny Burkstrom, Helena Burnett, Rick and Mary Catherine Dobson, Jacob Selvin, Rupert Emerley, Paul Buchanan, Marc and Ann Talbot, Lisa Voss, Peter and Kathleen Lloyd, Tim and Stacy Donnally, Charles Cortez, Joanne Jacobson, Tab Quisenberry, Julie Cummings, Matthew Conner, Paula Mitchell, Janet Burns, Michael Combs, Paula Mitchell, Sol Shapiro, Rick Poland, Tom Roberts, Wes Caplinger, Ben Caperton, Sissy Mills, Tucker Mayfield, Rev. Benson Hopper, India Michaelson, C. M. Gatton, Esther Parker, Dr. Lambert Lipscomb, Liz Murfree, Shelley Mellow, Rhoda Rettings, John Colbert, Mildred Cooney, Gates Borman, Lennie Maxwell, Maj. Blakeley Broadhurst, Carter Swain, Hazel Prince, Blanche DeSoto, Ed and Pamela Stubblefield, Helen Naismith, Dennis Custer, Scott Turnbull, Stephanie Lindsey, Fred O'Brien, Craig Biggart, Ed Hollas, Terrence Bainbridge, Al Cunningham, Lassiter Bowling, Suzanne Bracey, Robert Gross, Jarvis Jefferson, Lynn MacDermott, Randall Youngblood, Hilda Grayson, Maynard Pembroke, Trisha Everly, Lisa Garvin, Don Spain, Judith Rivers, Lori Murphy, Bill Beckman, Ted Armsley, Winnie Cassady, Harold Boxwell, Philip

Pershing, E. G. Falkner, Lester Beauregard, O. C. Ramsey, Opal Ellis, Emily Donovan, Julie Ottinger, Jon Purnell, Arthur Singer, Al Peterson, Walt Weberman, Lee Wong, Teenie Oakes, Wayne Stefan, Lester Short, Nate Henderson, Rod Guge, Lorene Denton, Ben Jacobs, Charles Talbert, Flo Reeves, Sam Levine, Mary Beth Simpson, Charlene Betts, Dale Diamond, Lillian Hartford, Noel McCambridge, Carolyn Bally, Dot Oldfield, Myra Sachs, Clyde Morrow, John Darwin, Jennifer Trumbull, Tom Glassman, Larry Stone, Sue Head, Tricia Cummings, Bill Dreher, Eddie Tornquist, Vernon Redfield, Hank Holder, Estelle Farmer, Terry Hawkins, Vance Aldridge, Helene Ashley, Avery Barnes, C. C. Cash, DeWitt Berryman, Greg O'Toole, E. J. Volksman, Rod Milliken, Melinda Powers, Dede Marcus, E. M. Cheek, Tim Frickas, Phyllis Turner, Horace and Sarah Brown, Eloise Hensley, Louis Ripley, Shorty Thomas, Mary Beth McKinney, Sam Dennison, Daniel O'Donnell, Boris Beaman, Ruth Van Sykes, Chelly Fuson, Howard Stennis, Barbara Abernathy, Mabel Ruleman, Graham Waltham, Louise Redmon, Cecily Radnor, Linda LeFevre, Jay Sanders, Barry Oberlin, Brad Sprague, Max Draper, Dorothy Corbitt, Janette Hensley, Hunter Hastings, Pauline Espy, Ingrid Otterman, Caroline Raines, Randall Towers, Dwight Evans, Foster Francis, Brooke Schumacher, Tommy Cooper, Roger Bolding, Lee Ann Pasquo, Fern Williamson, Jackie Mayo, Albert Alvarez, Chip Thomas, Marietta Schofield, Jeffrey Tree, Tom Hodges, Rob Thomas, James Otto, Ginger Gill, Edward Champion, Sam and Lane Suppa, Kate Hamilton, Benjamin Good, Thomas Fielder, Joe Boone, Betsy Porter, Walter Graves, Ted Bannister, Mariah Newhouse, Fred Hutchinson, Aubrey Lassiter, Allan Ward, Dinah Pearlstone, Al Skinner, Lou Crutcher, Jeffrey Reynolds, Terry Goodin, Charles Milam, Evelyn Nunnelly, Mario Minnelli, Beverlie Brewer, Ron Samuels, Kevin Ledbetter, M. S. Denby, Barry McAlister, Bob Seul,

Steve Knotts, Shiela Volkert, Darlene Harrell, Herman Goodman, Melody Greene, Jan Blaustone, Diana McLaughlin, Stewart Fairfax, Heidi Wallace, Kevin Carney, Samuel Stern, Phil and Marge Kidd, Amy Field, Millie Hedgpeth, Burt Brandenberg, Colin Darwin, Elizabeth Griffin, Lance Deekner, Haley and Paige Rumore, Susannah McGavock, Sallye Schumacher, Cissy French, Ben and Lauren Saks, Bob Mullins, Roy Hightower, Bettye Jean Matthews, Roberta Whitman, Elizabeth Becker, Ed Collings, Mae Daly, Myra Helms, Glen Hollanger, Jack Sims, Helen Goodbody, Col. Williams MacLeod, Margaret Longino, Manley Briggs, Malcolm Ellington, Timothy Clark, Frank Cavenaugh, Joanne Copeland, Stan and Melisssa Crane, Vernon Quinlen, Rudy Kipp, Todd Batson, Olga Martindale, B. C. Lang, Tex Thompson, Gertrude Brown, Bill Satterwhite, Jim Ratcliff, Grace Weinstein, Red Cooley, Joyce Choate, Joe Lusky, W. D. McMurray, J. J. Rogers, Capt. R. V. Carleton, Judy Goins, David Goodman, Debbie Wallace Craig, Leigh Webster, Curtis Solo, C. A. Craig II, Tricia Holt, Dennis Taylor, Anne Overton, Casey O'Brien, Tim Schwendimann, Scott and Laurie Head, Effie Jones, Michael Spears, Carol Lockhart, Mary Bousman, Eileen Mitchell, Paul Jay, Kim Chandler, Sol Heller, Bud Walters, Alexandria Main, Deidre Maddux, Katie, Blair, and Brien Rowan, Herb Kneeland, Addison Gore, Lisa Jones, Karen Freeman, Gertrude Brown, Doc Cline, Jill Martin, Martha DuBose, Owen Corello, Corinne Hall, Steven Yoo, Richard Speight, Richelle Melde, Meredith Ludwig, Nikole Mastroianni, Hollye Schumacher, Amy Zinman, Karl Weinmeister, Julie Levenberg, Paula Thompson, Kenneth Likely, Bonnie Smith, Doug Cooper, Beth Nicholson, Mitch Walters, John Burrows, Don Moore III, Ben Wilson, Anne Washburn, Shelby Applebaum, Sheri Tower, Bonnie Morales, Edwin C. Hoover.

To Rosemary and Adam

Other books by H. Jackson Brown, Jr.

A FATHER'S BOOK OF WISDOM
P.S. I LOVE YOU
LIFE'S LITTLE INSTRUCTION BOOK

I've learned that deciding whom you marry is the most important decision you'll ever make. —*Age 95*

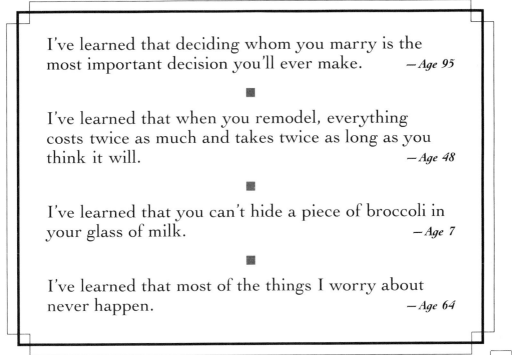

I've learned that when you remodel, everything costs twice as much and takes twice as long as you think it will. —*Age 48*

I've learned that you can't hide a piece of broccoli in your glass of milk. —*Age 7*

I've learned that most of the things I worry about never happen. —*Age 64*

I've learned that if someone says something unkind about me, I must live so that no one will believe it.

—Age 39

I've learned that a patrol car behind me always makes me nervous.

—Age 25

I've learned that every great achievement was once considered impossible.

—Age 47

I've learned that homemade Toll House cookies should be eaten while still warm.

—Age 29

I've learned that you can get by on charm for about fifteen minutes. After that, you'd better know something.
                                                                                                              —Age 46

I've learned that no one has a clue about what the stock market is going to do.
                                                                                                              —Age 51

I've learned that if you spread the peas out on your plate, it looks like you ate more.
                                                                                                              —Age 6

I've learned that couples without children always know just how you should raise yours.
                                                                                                              —Age 29

I've learned that the great challenge of life is to decide what's important and to disregard everything else.
                                                                    —Age 51

I've learned that getting fired can be the best thing that can happen to you.
                                                                    —Age 42

I've learned that just when I get my room the way I like it, Mom makes me clean it up.
                                                                    —Age 13

I've learned that almost no quality product sells for a cheap price.
                                                                    —Age 52

I've learned that you shouldn't compare yourself to the best others can do, but to the best you can do.

—Age 68

I've learned that the more creative you are, the more things you notice.

—Age 51

I've learned that you should never be too busy to say "please" and "thank you."

—Age 36

I've learned that you can't be a hero without taking chances.

—Age 43

I've learned that a person is only as good as his or her word. — *Age 90*

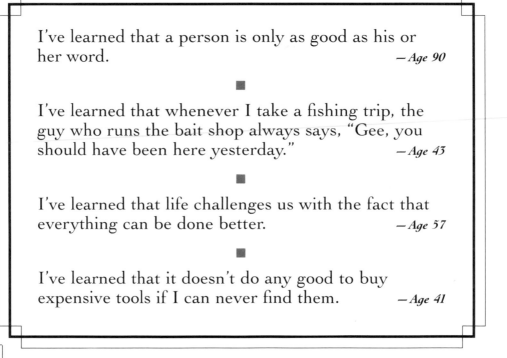

I've learned that whenever I take a fishing trip, the guy who runs the bait shop always says, "Gee, you should have been here yesterday." — *Age 43*

I've learned that life challenges us with the fact that everything can be done better. — *Age 57*

I've learned that it doesn't do any good to buy expensive tools if I can never find them. — *Age 41*

I've learned that good advice is hard to give but even harder to follow. —*Age 68*

I've learned that if chewing gum has been dropped on the sidewalk within the past 48 hours, my shoes will find it. —*Age 28*

I've learned that money is a lousy means of keeping score. —*Age 71*

I've learned that a strong code of ethics is as reliable as a compass. —*Age 43*

I've learned that if you like garlic salt and Tabasco sauce you can make almost anything taste good.

—Age 52

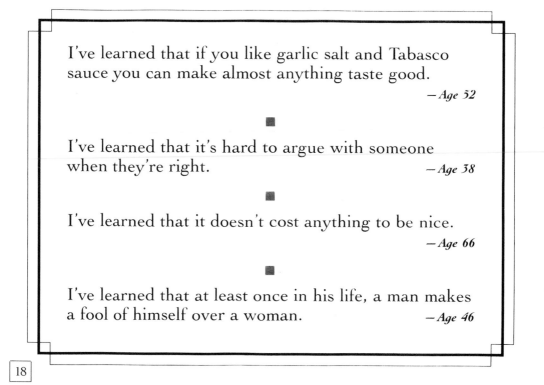

I've learned that it's hard to argue with someone when they're right.

—Age 38

I've learned that it doesn't cost anything to be nice.

—Age 66

I've learned that at least once in his life, a man makes a fool of himself over a woman.

—Age 46

I've learned that trust is the single most important factor in both personal and professional relationships.

—Age 20

I've learned that marrying for money is the hardest way of getting it.

—Age 42

I've learned that my gas tank is always on empty when I'm late for an important meeting.

—Age 32

I've learned that nothing of value comes without effort.

—Age 64

I've learned that you can be in love with four girls at the same time.
                                                                — Age 9

I've learned that even the simplest task can be meaningful if I do it in the right spirit.
                                                                — Age 72

I've learned that you can tell a lot about a man by the happiness of his wife and the respect given him by his children.
                                                                — Age 51

I've learned that lying in the green grass of an empty field makes you feel so good.
                                                                — Age 14

I've learned that it's better to be married to someone with a good nature than a good physique. — *Age 39*

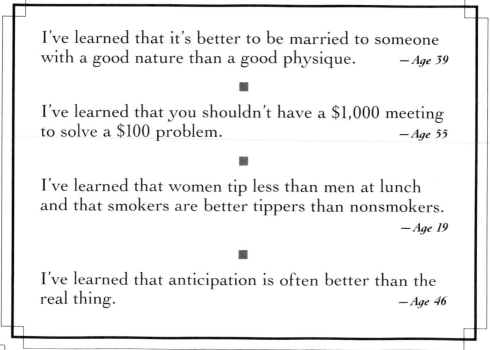

I've learned that you shouldn't have a $1,000 meeting to solve a $100 problem. — *Age 55*

I've learned that women tip less than men at lunch and that smokers are better tippers than nonsmokers. — *Age 19*

I've learned that anticipation is often better than the real thing. — *Age 46*

I've learned that enthusiasm is caught, not taught.

—Age 51

I've learned that whenever I decide something with kindness, I usually make the right decision. *—Age 66*

I've learned that you need to let your children be children. *—Age 38*

I've learned that in every face-to-face encounter, regardless of how brief, we leave something behind.

—Age 45

I've learned that if you hire mediocre people, they will hire mediocre people.
—Age 55

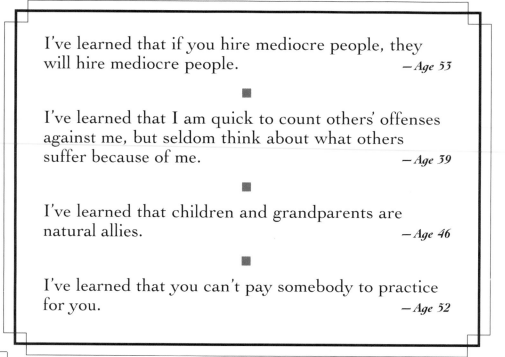

I've learned that I am quick to count others' offenses against me, but seldom think about what others suffer because of me.
—Age 39

I've learned that children and grandparents are natural allies.
—Age 46

I've learned that you can't pay somebody to practice for you.
—Age 52

I've learned that even when you schedule a doctor's appointment at 8:00 A.M., you still have to wait an hour.   —*Age 42*

I've learned that you can do something in an instant that will give you a heartache for life.   —*Age 27*

I've learned that a teenager's biggest fear is the fear of a broken heart.   —*Age 16*

I've learned that even when I have pains, I don't have to be a pain.   —*Age 82*

I've learned that I shouldn't go grocery shopping when I'm hungry.
— *Age 38*

I've learned that one of the sweetest smells I know is my husband's clean-shaven face in the morning.
— *Age 39*

I've learned that car salesmen size up prospects by looking at their shoes and watches.
— *Age 52*

I've learned that if I'm in trouble at school, I'm in more trouble at home.
— *Age 11*

I've learned that people who wear Mickey Mouse
watches are usually creative and fun to be with.

—Age 33

I've learned that no matter how thin you slice it,
there are always two sides. *—Age 58*

I've learned that regardless of color or age, we all
need about the same amount of love. *—Age 37*

I've learned that a person's degree of self-confidence
greatly determines his success. *—Age 42*

I've learned that people allow themselves to be only as successful as they think they deserve to be. —*Age 50*

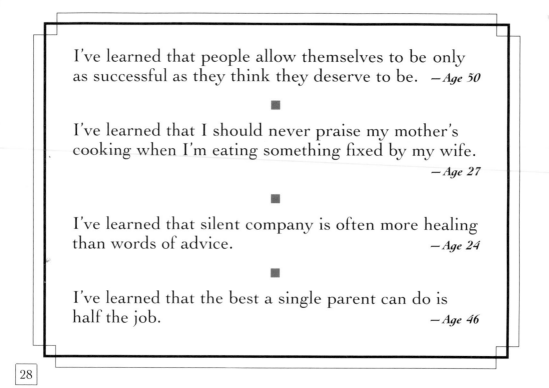

I've learned that I should never praise my mother's cooking when I'm eating something fixed by my wife.

—*Age 27*

I've learned that silent company is often more healing than words of advice. —*Age 24*

I've learned that the best a single parent can do is half the job. —*Age 46*

I've learned that you can't hug your kids too much.

—Age 54

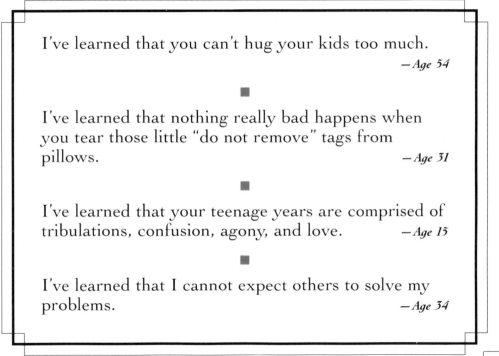

I've learned that nothing really bad happens when you tear those little "do not remove" tags from pillows.

—Age 31

I've learned that your teenage years are comprised of tribulations, confusion, agony, and love.

—Age 15

I've learned that I cannot expect others to solve my problems.

—Age 34

I've learned that if you pursue happiness, it will elude you. But if you focus on your family, the needs of others, your work, meeting new people, and doing the very best you can, happiness will find you. —*Age 65*

I've learned that motel mattresses are better on the side away from the phone. —*Age 50*

I've learned that it makes me sad when I'm the last one chosen for a team. —*Age 9*

I've learned that if you care, it shows. —*Age 30*

I've learned that eating chocolate won't solve your problems, but it doesn't hurt anything either.   *—Age 28*

I've learned that animals can sometimes warm your heart better than people can.   *—Age 15*

I've learned that kindness is more important than perfection.   *—Age 70*

I've learned that regardless of your relationship with your parents, you miss them terribly after they die.

—Age 53

I've learned that if you take good care of your employees, they will take good care of your customers.
—Age 49

I've learned that you should never go to bed with an argument unsettled.
—Age 73

I've learned that nothing is more fun than a job you enjoy.
—Age 29

I've learned that education, experience, and memories are three things no one can take away from you.
—Age 67

I've learned that you should always take time to answer young children when they ask "why?" *—Age 28*

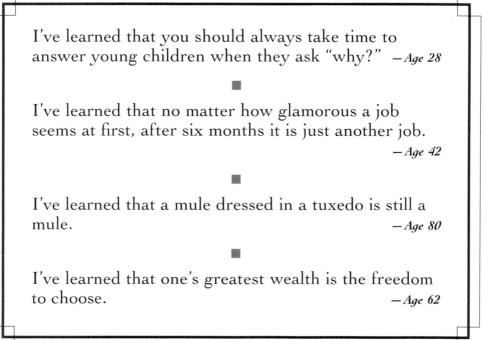

I've learned that no matter how glamorous a job seems at first, after six months it is just another job.

—Age 42

I've learned that a mule dressed in a tuxedo is still a mule. *—Age 80*

I've learned that one's greatest wealth is the freedom to choose. *—Age 62*

I've learned that it's taking me a long time to become the person I want to be. *—Age 51*

I've learned that you shouldn't look back except to learn. *—Age 70*

I've learned that Mom wouldn't like my boyfriend even if he were captain of the football team and sang in the church choir. *—Age 17*

I've learned that the best way to lose a friend is to lend him money. *—Age 36*

I've learned that when your husband cooks, you should compliment everything he fixes. — *Age 77*

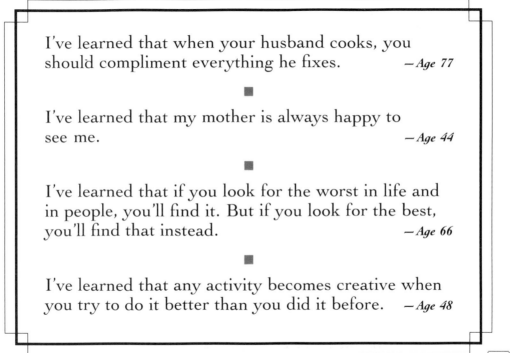

I've learned that my mother is always happy to see me. — *Age 44*

I've learned that if you look for the worst in life and in people, you'll find it. But if you look for the best, you'll find that instead. — *Age 66*

I've learned that any activity becomes creative when you try to do it better than you did it before. — *Age 48*

I've learned that more comfort doesn't necessarily mean more happiness.
—Age 55

I've learned that the greater a person's sense of guilt, the greater his need to cast blame on others.
—Age 46

I've learned that self-pity is a waste of time.
—Age 81

I've learned that when traveling overseas, it's best to carry a good supply of American-made toilet paper.
—Age 54

I've learned that my children's birthdays make me
feel older than my own birthday does.   —Age 46

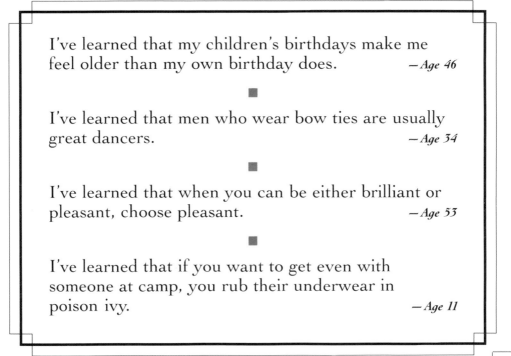

I've learned that men who wear bow ties are usually
great dancers.   —Age 34

I've learned that when you can be either brilliant or
pleasant, choose pleasant.   —Age 53

I've learned that if you want to get even with
someone at camp, you rub their underwear in
poison ivy.   —Age 11

I've learned that the secret of growing old gracefully is never to lose your enthusiasm for meeting new people and seeing new places. *—Age 75*

I've learned that you can't tell how far a frog can jump just by looking at him. *—Age 79*

I've learned that generous people seldom have emotional and mental problems. *—Age 51*

I've learned that it's a lot easier to react than it is to think. *—Age 55*

I've learned that it is very painful to see my negative
personality traits alive in my children.   —*Age 39*

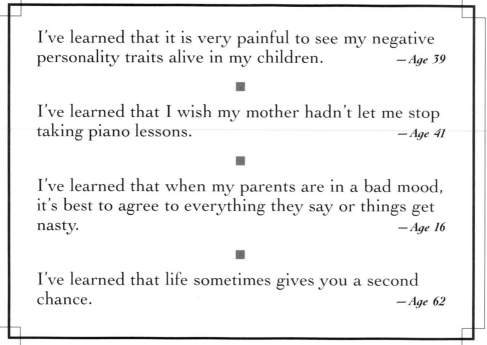

I've learned that I wish my mother hadn't let me stop
taking piano lessons.   —*Age 41*

I've learned that when my parents are in a bad mood,
it's best to agree to everything they say or things get
nasty.   —*Age 16*

I've learned that life sometimes gives you a second
chance.   —*Age 62*

I've learned that when I drop a slice of bread with jelly on it, it always lands jelly-side down. —*Age 33*

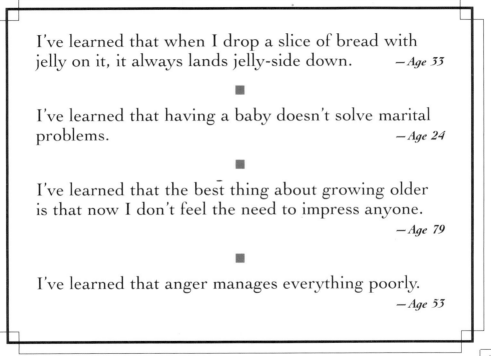

I've learned that having a baby doesn't solve marital problems. —*Age 24*

I've learned that the best thing about growing older is that now I don't feel the need to impress anyone.

—*Age 79*

I've learned that anger manages everything poorly.

—*Age 53*

I've learned that the size of your biceps has very little to do with your popularity and success after high school.
—*Age 50*

■

I've learned that the worst pain is watching someone else in pain.
—*Age 46*

■

I've learned that it pays to believe in miracles. And to tell the truth, I've seen several.
—*Age 73*

■

I've learned that if your children feel safe, wanted, and loved, you are a successful parent.
—*Age 39*

I've learned that if you're riding in a pickup truck with two other people, you should either drive or sit in the middle. The person riding shotgun has to get out to open and close all the gates. — *Age 19*

I've learned that when someone tells you it's the principle of the thing and not the money, it's usually the money. — *Age 65*

I've learned that violence on television and in the movies is so graphic and extreme that it's numbing our children to pain and suffering in the real world.

— *Age 59*

I've learned that if you give a pig and a boy everything they want, you'll get a good pig and a bad boy. —*Age 77*

I've learned that nothing is more soothing than the warm sun on your face. —*Age 29*

I've learned that some money costs too much. —*Age 51*

I've learned that attractiveness is a positive, caring attitude and has nothing to do with face lifts or nose jobs. —*Age 56*

I've learned that there's no substitute for good
manners.   *— Age 37*

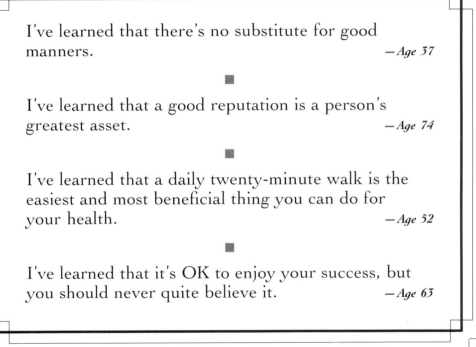

I've learned that a good reputation is a person's
greatest asset.   *— Age 74*

I've learned that a daily twenty-minute walk is the
easiest and most beneficial thing you can do for
your health.   *— Age 52*

I've learned that it's OK to enjoy your success, but
you should never quite believe it.   *— Age 63*

I've learned that you shouldn't look for romance where you work.

—*Age 31*

I've learned that everyone is attractive when they smile.

—*Age 51*

I've learned that although parents and elders may lecture and discipline you, you will later realize that it was because they cared.

—*Age 15*

I've learned that if you laugh and drink soda pop at the same time, it will come out your nose.

—*Age 7*

I've learned that if you read something that's unintelligible gibberish, it was probably written by a lawyer. *—Age 48*

I've learned that parenthood isn't as scary as I thought it would be. *—Age 22*

I've learned that you never really know your friends until you take a vacation with them. *—Age 41*

I've learned that "call waiting" deserves to be included among the planet's greatest abominations. *—Age 55*

I've learned that when traveling the interstates in Ohio, it's best to observe the speed limit. *—Age 41*

I've learned that a sunroof is worth the extra cost. *—Age 29*

I've learned that you should always leave loved ones with loving words. It could be the last time you see them. *—Age 60*

I've learned that brushing my child's hair is one of life's great pleasures. *—Age 29*

I've learned that even a doctor with the best training and intentions can be wrong about a diagnosis.

—Age 58

I've learned that wealthy people are no happier than those of modest means. *—Age 68*

I've learned that wherever I go, the world's worst drivers have followed me there. *—Age 29*

I've learned that it's better not to wait for a crisis to discover what's important in your life. *—Age 45*

I've learned that the person with big dreams is more powerful than one with all the facts. —*Age 51*

I've learned that I do not have to be perfect all the time for my family to love me. —*Age 18*

I've learned that I should make the little decisions with my head and the big decisions with my heart.

—*Age 52*

I've learned that it's best not to quit at quitting time.

—*Age 37*

I've learned that you should never pay for a job until it's completed. *—Age 48*

I've learned that people are about as happy as they decide to be. *—Age 79*

I've learned that when you read bedtime stories, kids really do notice if you use the same voice for the handsome prince that you used for the evil ogre the night before. *—Age 29*

I've learned that most people are honest. *—Age 82*

I've learned that the best and quickest way to appreciate other people is to try and do their job.

—Age 51

I've learned that it's easier to stay out of trouble than to get out of trouble.

—Age 14

I've learned that if your life is free of failures, you're probably not taking enough risks.

—Age 42

I've learned that days are long, but life is short.

—Age 88

I've learned that when you have the choice of eating at a table or at the counter in a coffee shop, choose the counter. The service will be faster, the food hotter, and the conversation livelier. —*Age 46*

I've learned that there are four ages of men:
(1) when you believe in Santa Claus, (2) when you don't believe in Santa Claus, (3) when you are Santa Claus, and (4) when you look like Santa Claus.

—*Age 51*

I've learned that singing "Amazing Grace" can lift my spirits for hours. —*Age 49*

I've learned that "Today's Featured Items" is a euphemism for "Things We Need To Get Rid Of."

—Age 19

I've learned that being a success at the office is not worth it if it means being a failure at home. *—Age 51*

I've learned that there's nothing you can't teach yourself by reading. *—Age 78*

I've learned that humming a tune when you're upset can ease your mind. *—Age 14*

I've learned that children are the best teachers of creativity, persistence, and unconditional love. *—Age 37*

I've learned that you learn most from people who are learning themselves. *—Age 62*

I've learned that when Mommy and Daddy shout at each other, it scares me. *—Age 5*

I've learned that when bad times come, you can let them make you bitter or use them to make you better. *—Age 75*

I've learned that encouragement from a good teacher can turn a student's life around. —*Age 44*

■

I've learned that the simple things are often the most satisfying. —*Age 63*

■

I've learned that when my daddy kisses me in the mornings, he smells like a piece of Jolly Rancher candy. —*Age 10*

■

I've learned that you should never sign a contract with blank spaces. —*Age 47*

I've learned that if love isn't taught in the home, it's difficult to learn it anywhere else. — *Age 51*

I've learned that when I eat fish sticks, they help me swim faster because they're fish. — *Age 7*

I've learned that you can make someone's day by simply sending them a little card. — *Age 44*

I've learned that women with double first names usually know how to make terrific peach cobbler.

— *Age 29*

I've learned that to experience the wonder of life through the eyes of a child is the most rewarding feeling in the world. *—Age 30*

I've learned that there are no unimportant acts of kindness. *—Age 51*

I've learned that I don't feel my age as long as I focus on my dreams instead of on my regrets. *—Age 83*

I've learned that nothing tastes as good as vegetables from your own garden. *—Age 62*

I've learned that to love and be loved is the greatest joy in the world. *—Age 78*

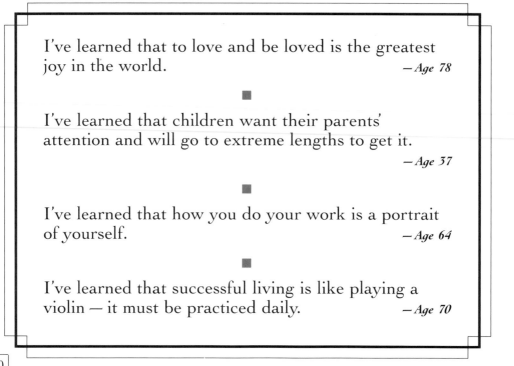

I've learned that children want their parents' attention and will go to extreme lengths to get it. *—Age 37*

I've learned that how you do your work is a portrait of yourself. *—Age 64*

I've learned that successful living is like playing a violin — it must be practiced daily. *—Age 70*

I've learned that in the stock market, bulls make money and bears make money, but hogs get slaughtered.
—Age 45

■

I've learned that you shouldn't marry someone who has more problems than you.
—Age 31

■

I've learned that when I grow up, I'm going to be an artist. It's in my blood.
—Age 8

■

I've learned that you never ask a lady her age, her weight, or what's in her purse.
—Age 68

I've learned that it's just as important to forget a wrong as it is to remember a kindness. — *Age 72*

I've learned that if I don't try new things, I won't learn new things. — *Age 38*

I've learned that if you wait until retirement to really start living, you've waited too long. — *Age 67*

I've learned that when making a decision, **no** is more easily changed to **yes** than **yes** is changed to **no**.

— *Age 55*

I've learned that when you judge others, you are revealing your own fears and prejudices. —*Age 49*

I've learned that when I wave to people in the country, they stop what they're doing and wave back.

—*Age 9*

I've learned that when things go wrong, I don't have to go with them. —*Age 72*

I've learned that debt is a poor substitute for what it buys. —*Age 58*

I've learned that I can't change the past, but I can let it go. —*Age 63*

I've learned that total pleasure is a good book, a soft couch, and a cat curled up beside you. —*Age 50*

I've learned that you can't judge boys by the way they look. —*Age 12*

I've learned that if you keep doing what you've always done, you'll keep getting what you've always gotten. —*Age 51*

I've learned that, ultimately, takers lose and givers win. —*Age 58*

I've learned that if you want to cheer up yourself, you should try cheering up someone else. —*Age 13*

I've learned that a full life is not determined by how long you live, but by how well. —*Age 66*

I've learned that you should never jump out of a second story window using a sheet for a parachute. —*Age 10*

I've learned that good health is true wealth. *—Age 77*

I've learned that to become successful, it helps to dress the part. *—Age 28*

I've learned that even small children have a right to privacy. *—Age 33*

I've learned that when you have an argument with your spouse, the first one who says, "I'm sorry I hurt your feelings; please forgive me," is the winner.

—Age 51

I've learned that the person who says something can't be done is often interrupted by someone doing it.

—Age 43

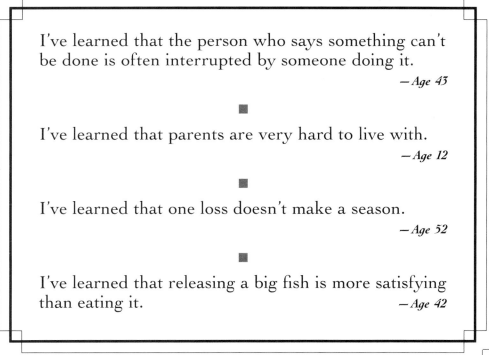

I've learned that parents are very hard to live with.

—Age 12

I've learned that one loss doesn't make a season.

—Age 52

I've learned that releasing a big fish is more satisfying than eating it.

—Age 42

I've learned that milk tastes best when drunk straight
out of the plastic jug.   *—Age 48*

I've learned that every time I'm on a trip I wish I
were home, and every time I'm at home I wish I were
on a trip.   *—Age 59*

I've learned that optimists live longer than pessimists.
That's why I'm an optimist.   *—Age 84*

I've learned that although it's hard to admit it, I'm
secretly glad my parents are strict with me.   *—Age 15*

I've learned that there are two things essential to a happy marriage — separate checking accounts and separate bathrooms. *—Age 36*

I've learned that you should treat everyone with respect, and demand respect in return. *—Age 51*

I've learned that my best friends are usually the ones who get me in trouble. *—Age 11*

I've learned that you can keep going long after you think you can't. *—Age 69*

I've learned that it's disastrous to forget your anniversary.
                                            —*Age 44*

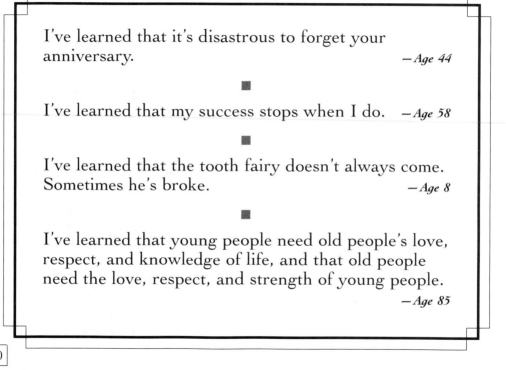

I've learned that my success stops when I do. —*Age 58*

I've learned that the tooth fairy doesn't always come. Sometimes he's broke.
                                            —*Age 8*

I've learned that young people need old people's love, respect, and knowledge of life, and that old people need the love, respect, and strength of young people.
                                            —*Age 85*

I've learned that leisure is not enjoyed unless it has been earned. — *Age 51*

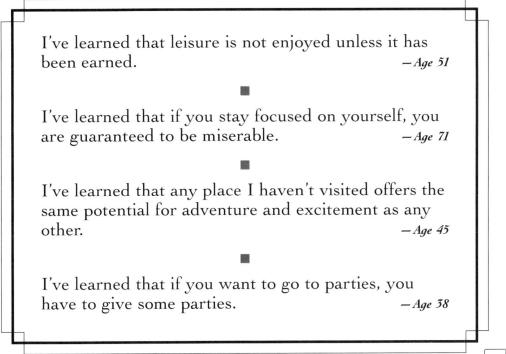

I've learned that if you stay focused on yourself, you are guaranteed to be miserable. — *Age 71*

I've learned that any place I haven't visited offers the same potential for adventure and excitement as any other. — *Age 45*

I've learned that if you want to go to parties, you have to give some parties. — *Age 38*

I've learned that the wealthy person is the one who's content with what he has. —*Age 61*

I've learned that no one can keep a secret. —*Age 17*

I've learned that you can ruin a good relationship with a professional person such as a doctor, a lawyer, or a CPA when you assume he or she wants to talk shop after hours. —*Age 40*

I've learned that everyone has something to teach. —*Age 51*

I've learned that I have never regretted being
too generous, but often regretted not being
generous enough.   *—Age 76*

I've learned that spite is a boomerang even if it's
never acted out.   *—Age 46*

I've learned that you should keep your promises no
matter what.   *—Age 81*

I've learned that regardless of which bank teller's line
you get in, the other ones move faster. *—Age 32*

I've learned that love will break your heart, but it's worth it.
—Age 26

I've learned that categorizing people is destructive and unfair.
—Age 39

I've learned that as long as I have my health, older is better than younger.
—Age 72

I've learned that if you talk on the phone too long with a girl, your parents suspect something is going on.
—Age 11

I've learned that to insure rain, schedule an outdoor wedding.

—Age 52

I've learned that I can't tell the difference between a $20 bottle of wine and a $40 bottle of wine.

—Age 39

I've learned that I love my brother because he sticks up for me.

—Age 9

I've learned that if you are the boss and you stop rowing, you shouldn't be surprised if everyone else rests too.

—Age 59

I've learned that everyone can afford to be generous with praise. It's not something available only to the well-to-do. —*Age 76*

■

I've learned that what you are thinking about, you are becoming. —*Age 55*

■

I've learned that it's harmful for parents to live out their athletic fantasies through their children. —*Age 43*

■

I've learned that a person's posture says a lot about his or her self-confidence. —*Age 59*

I've learned that I will always be seeking my parents' approval.
 — *Age 39*

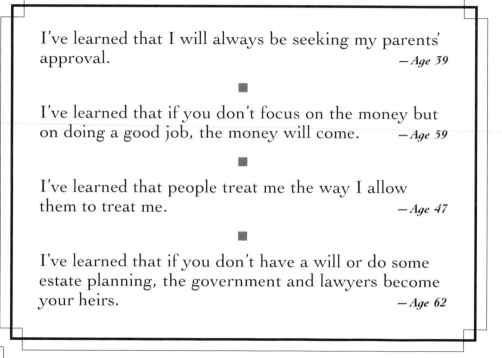

I've learned that if you don't focus on the money but on doing a good job, the money will come.
 — *Age 59*

I've learned that people treat me the way I allow them to treat me.
 — *Age 47*

I've learned that if you don't have a will or do some estate planning, the government and lawyers become your heirs.
 — *Age 62*

I've learned that parents will never understand the importance of a telephone to a teenager. —*Age 16*

I've learned that whatever I love to do, I do well.

—*Age 48*

I've learned that when someone hurts your feelings, it's unimportant unless you persist in remembering it.

—*Age 68*

I've learned that when giving advice, it's best to make it brief. —*Age 80*

I've learned that my greatest fear is that in later years I'll look back at a long list of things I "never got around to." —*Age 30*

■

I've learned that what my grandmother said was true: time does seem to go faster the older you get. —*Age 48*

■

I've learned that girls sweat just as much as boys.

—*Age 11*

■

I've learned that if I don't know the answer, it's best to say, "I don't know." —*Age 59*

I've learned that it takes a lot more creativity to find out what's right than what's wrong. — *Age 38*

I've learned that if a child is not getting love and attention at home, he will go somewhere else to find them. — *Age 46*

I've learned that you shouldn't brag about one of your children in the presence of another. — *Age 77*

I've learned that expensive new silk ties are the only ones that attract spaghetti sauce. — *Age 44*

I've learned that I should never try out a new recipe
on guests.   *—Age 24*

I've learned that all transactions and relationships are
enriched by courtesy.   *—Age 59*

I've learned that I don't make many mistakes with my
mouth shut.   *—Age 33*

I've learned that beyond a certain comfortable style
of living, the more material things you have, the less
freedom you have.   *—Age 62*

I've learned that an insatiable curiosity is important to never feeling old. — *Age 71*

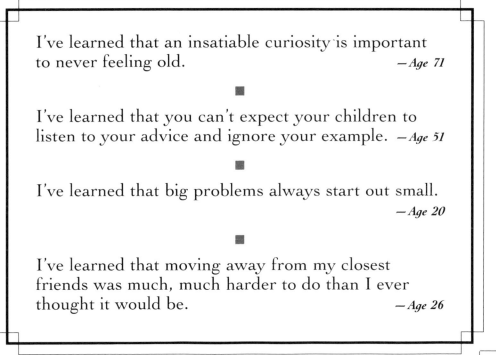

I've learned that you can't expect your children to listen to your advice and ignore your example. — *Age 51*

I've learned that big problems always start out small. — *Age 20*

I've learned that moving away from my closest friends was much, much harder to do than I ever thought it would be. — *Age 26*

I've learned that happiness is like perfume: you can't give it away without getting a little on yourself.

—Age 59

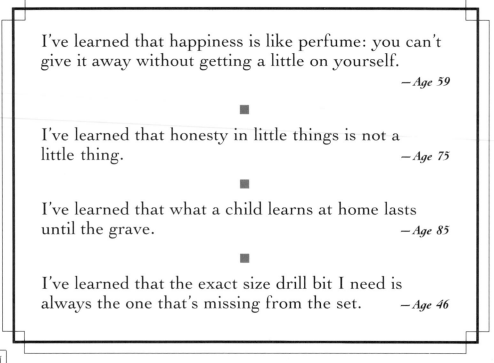

I've learned that honesty in little things is not a little thing.

—Age 75

I've learned that what a child learns at home lasts until the grave.

—Age 85

I've learned that the exact size drill bit I need is always the one that's missing from the set.

—Age 46

I've learned that the dashing young knight on his snow white steed who was going to ride into my life and sweep me off my feet has apparently gotten lost in the forest.

—Age 46

I've learned that there is something more painful than hate. It's indifference.

—Age 62

I've learned that goldfish don't like Jell-O.

—Age 5

I've learned that work enjoyed is as much fun as leisure.

—Age 51

I've learned that being a grandparent is God's compensation for growing older. — *Age 64*

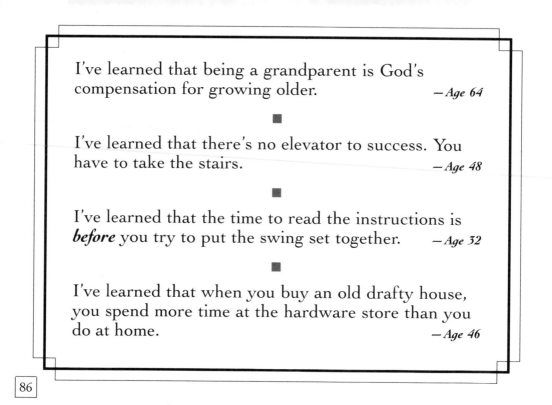

I've learned that there's no elevator to success. You have to take the stairs. — *Age 48*

I've learned that the time to read the instructions is **before** you try to put the swing set together. — *Age 32*

I've learned that when you buy an old drafty house, you spend more time at the hardware store than you do at home. — *Age 46*

I've learned that joining the family business was a big mistake.
—Age 34

I've learned that you should treasure your children for what they are, not for what you want them to be.
—Age 39

I've learned that the only thing you owe life is to become the best you can be.
—Age 31

I've learned that it's best to buy the expensive paint that covers in one coat.
—Age 29

I've learned that if your mother made pimiento cheese with Miracle Whip, you don't like it when it's made with mayonnaise. —*Age 32*

I've learned that although there may be reasons to be cynical, it never helps correct the situation. —*Age 51*

I've learned that if you smile at people, they will almost always smile back. —*Age 81*

I've learned that it's easier to *keep* up than to *catch* up. —*Age 46*

I've learned that being too quick to judge someone can deprive you of a great encounter and the possibility of a wonderful long-term relationship.

—Age 40

I've learned that I have never been bored in the presence of a cheerful person. *—Age 63*

I've learned that we are responsible for what we do, no matter how we feel. *—Age 51*

I've learned that the IRS makes mistakes. *—Age 38*

I've learned that I can't visit a bookstore without buying something. —*Age 44*

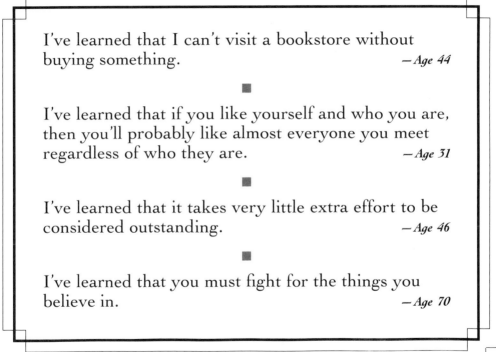

I've learned that if you like yourself and who you are, then you'll probably like almost everyone you meet regardless of who they are. —*Age 31*

I've learned that it takes very little extra effort to be considered outstanding. —*Age 46*

I've learned that you must fight for the things you believe in. —*Age 70*

I've learned that when I'm late for work, that's the one morning my boss is early. — *Age 38*

I've learned that my children expect as much from me as I expect from them. — *Age 51*

I've learned that when I come home from a date, it always makes me feel good to see that my parents have left the porch light on for me. — *Age 17*

I've learned that age is important only if you are a cheese. — *Age 76*

I've learned that if you put marital problems on the back burner, they are sure to boil over. *—Age 66*

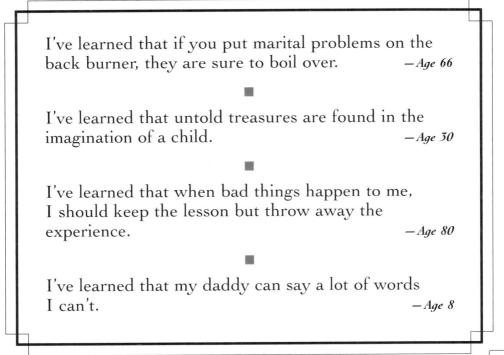

I've learned that untold treasures are found in the imagination of a child. *—Age 30*

I've learned that when bad things happen to me, I should keep the lesson but throw away the experience. *—Age 80*

I've learned that my daddy can say a lot of words I can't. *—Age 8*

I've learned that going the extra mile puts you miles ahead of your competition.
—Age 66

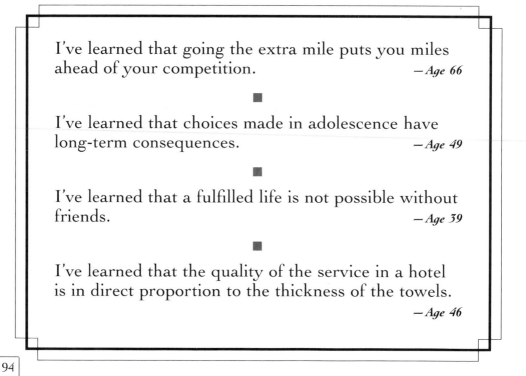

I've learned that choices made in adolescence have long-term consequences.
—Age 49

I've learned that a fulfilled life is not possible without friends.
—Age 39

I've learned that the quality of the service in a hotel is in direct proportion to the thickness of the towels.
—Age 46

I've learned that you should invest in your family first and in your career second. —*Age 48*

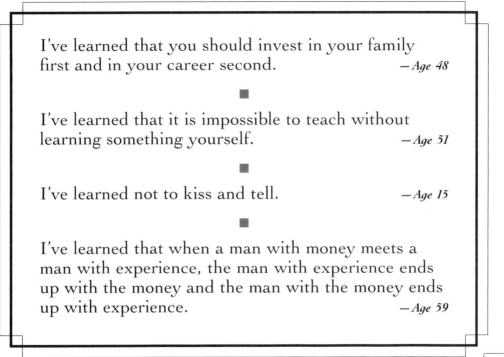

I've learned that it is impossible to teach without learning something yourself. —*Age 51*

I've learned not to kiss and tell. —*Age 15*

I've learned that when a man with money meets a man with experience, the man with experience ends up with the money and the man with the money ends up with experience. —*Age 59*

I've learned that no one makes potato salad as good as Mom's.
—Age 51

■

I've learned that if you depend on others to make you happy, you'll be endlessly disappointed.
—Age 60

■

I've learned that if there were no problems, there would be no opportunities.
—Age 19

■

I've learned that when wearing suspenders with one strap down, you need to be careful when going to the bathroom.
—Age 10

I've learned that you shouldn't fight a battle if there's nothing to win. —*Age 53*

I've learned that my mother sometimes laughs so hard she snorts. —*Age 7*

I've learned that everything sounds romantic in a foreign language, no matter what is said. —*Age 27*

I've learned that if you really want to do something positive for your children, you should try to improve your marriage. —*Age 61*

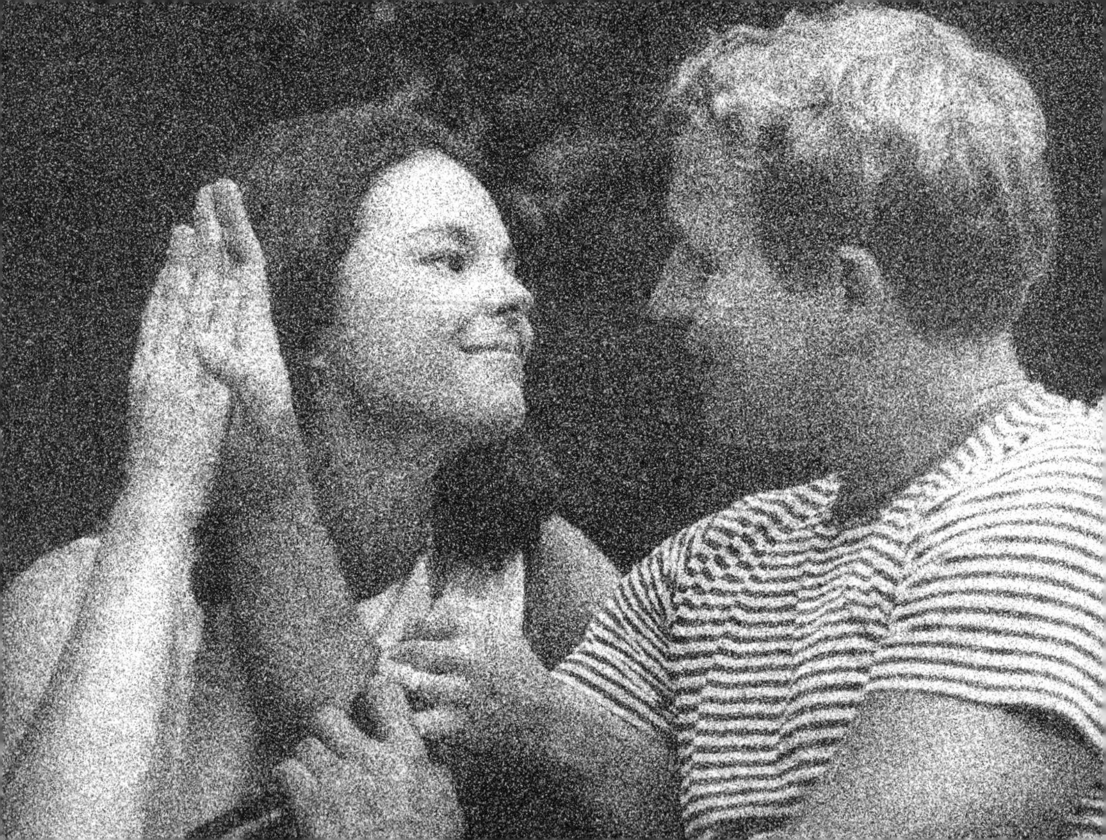

I've learned that you know your husband still loves you when there are two brownies left and he takes the smaller one. —*Age 39*

I've learned that the most creative ideas come from beginners — not the experts. —*Age 62*

I've learned that nothing gives you freedom like a few bucks in the bank. —*Age 48*

I've learned that if you can't forgive and forget, you can at least forgive and move on. —*Age 77*

I've learned that how people treat me is more a reflection of how they see themselves than how they see me.   —*Age 49*

I've learned that envy is the enemy of happiness.
                                                    —*Age 73*

I've learned that the purpose of criticism is to help, not to humiliate.   —*Age 49*

I've learned that making a living is not the same thing as making a life.   —*Age 58*

I've learned that nothing is more precious than a
baby's laugh. *—Age 29*

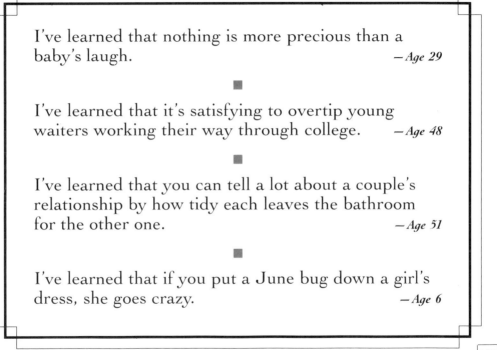

I've learned that it's satisfying to overtip young
waiters working their way through college. *—Age 48*

I've learned that you can tell a lot about a couple's
relationship by how tidy each leaves the bathroom
for the other one. *—Age 51*

I've learned that if you put a June bug down a girl's
dress, she goes crazy. *—Age 6*

I've learned that love is a great investment. No matter whom you give it to, it returns great dividends.

—Age 67

I've learned that middle age is the best time of my life — so far.

—Age 50

I've learned that you can't please some people, no matter what you do.

—Age 35

I've learned that it's impossible to take a ten-day vacation without gaining ten pounds.

—Age 55

I've learned that men and women can get intoxicated on power as easily as on alcohol. —*Age 53*

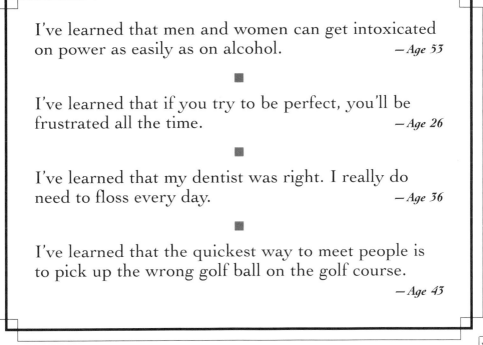

I've learned that if you try to be perfect, you'll be frustrated all the time. —*Age 26*

I've learned that my dentist was right. I really do need to floss every day. —*Age 36*

I've learned that the quickest way to meet people is to pick up the wrong golf ball on the golf course.

—*Age 43*

I've learned that if you want to get promoted, you must do things that get noticed. —*Age 54*

I've learned that the two happiest days of my life were the day I bought my boat and the day I sold my boat. —*Age 42*

I've learned that you shouldn't confuse a black crayon with a Tootsie Roll. —*Age 10*

I've learned that if you wait until all conditions are perfect before you act, you'll never act. —*Age 64*

I've learned that people will obey almost any reasonable request except, "Please remain seated until the captain has brought the aircraft to a complete stop at the gate." —*Age 51*

I've learned that you either control your attitude or it controls you. —*Age 47*

I've learned that success is more often the result of hard work than of talent. —*Age 59*

I've learned that everyone can use a prayer. —*Age 72*

I've learned that if there are things about your sweetheart that you don't admire, you will like them even less after you marry him. —*Age 25*

I've learned that the best advice you can give anyone is, "Be kind." —*Age 66*

I've learned that even the happiest people have down days. —*Age 27*

I've learned that inside every bad person is a good person trying to get out. —*Age 58*

I've learned that sometimes I just need to be held.

— Age 36

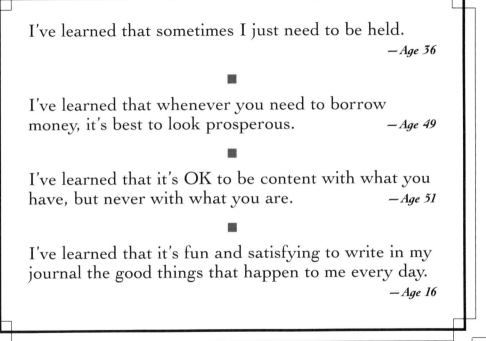

I've learned that whenever you need to borrow money, it's best to look prosperous.

— Age 49

I've learned that it's OK to be content with what you have, but never with what you are.

— Age 51

I've learned that it's fun and satisfying to write in my journal the good things that happen to me every day.

— Age 16

I've learned that a person's greatest need is to feel appreciated. *—Age 45*

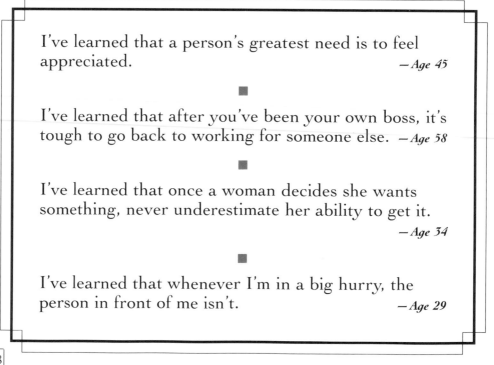

I've learned that after you've been your own boss, it's tough to go back to working for someone else. *—Age 58*

I've learned that once a woman decides she wants something, never underestimate her ability to get it. *—Age 34*

I've learned that whenever I'm in a big hurry, the person in front of me isn't. *—Age 29*

I've learned that if you want decent airline food, call ahead and ask for a low-sodium meal. It's always better than the regular fare. *—Age 42*

■

I've learned that you always find time to do the things you really want to do. *—Age 64*

■

I've learned that I would like to be a horse and live on a ranch, if only cowboys didn't wear spurs. *—Age 8*

■

I've learned that you shouldn't confuse success with usefulness. *—Age 51*

I've learned that regardless of how little you have, you can always give comfort and encouragement.

—Age 64

■

I've learned that the time I really need a vacation is when I'm just back from one.

—Age 38

■

I've learned that the greatest risk is in thinking too small.

—Age 61

■

I've learned that you should fill your life with experiences, not excuses.

—Age 51

I've learned that joy is often the ability to be happy in small ways. *—Age 72*

I've learned that a clean car drives better than a dirty one. *—Age 55*

I've learned that the older I get, the more pretty girls I remember kissing as a young man. *—Age 84*

I've learned that there is no way to make up for the time you should have spent with your children.

—Age 49

I've learned that a good feeling gets even better when it's shared.
—Age 14

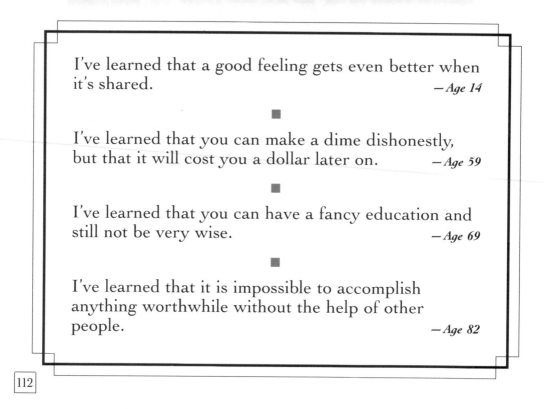

I've learned that you can make a dime dishonestly, but that it will cost you a dollar later on.
—Age 59

I've learned that you can have a fancy education and still not be very wise.
—Age 69

I've learned that it is impossible to accomplish anything worthwhile without the help of other people.
—Age 82

I've learned that I like my teacher because she cries when we sing "Silent Night."

—Age 7

I've learned that worry is often a substitute for action.

—Age 50

I've learned that regardless of how hot and steamy a relationship is at first, the passion fades and there had better be something else to take its place.

—Age 29

I've learned that people are never sneaky in only one area of their life.

—Age 40

I've learned that you can have fun regardless of how little money you have. When I was small, we didn't have enough money for a ball, and so we would wrap a rock with cotton, put it in a sock, and make our own ball.   *—Age 63*

I've learned that you should get all estimates in writing.   *—Age 35*

I've learned that regardless of what I've had for supper, I can't resist spooning a little peanut butter out of the jar before going to bed.   *—Age 48*

I've learned that Cokes taste better in the small bottles.

— Age 54

I've learned that people don't want advice, but understanding.

— Age 40

I've learned that you should make the money before you spend it.

— Age 48

I've learned that there comes a time when you must stop grieving over the death of a loved one and get on with your life.

— Age 67

I've learned that all women love to get flowers, especially when there's no particular reason. *—Age 33*

■

I've learned that heroes are the people who do what has to be done when it needs to be done, regardless of the consequences. *—Age 77*

■

I've learned that it's best to be decisive, even if it means I'll sometimes be wrong. *—Age 51*

■

I've learned that learning to forgive takes practice. *—Age 15*

I've learned that you never ask a tire salesman if you
need new tires.   *—Age 44*

I've learned that you shouldn't push your luck. Play
it safe and move the ladder.   *—Age 79*

I've learned that being a good mother is the best
occupation you can ever have.   *—Age 35*

I've learned that a good relationship between me and
my family, my friends, and my business associates
can be boiled down to one word: *respect.*   *—Age 56*

I've learned that there's no friend like an old friend, no dog like an old dog, and no money like old money.

—Age 74

I've learned that good things generally do happen to good people.

—Age 29

I've learned that you can't throw mud without getting a little on yourself.

—Age 66

I've learned that fourteen days is too long to spend on an ocean cruise.

—Age 49

I've learned that if there were ten people in a hayloft, I'd be the first to jump off.
— *Age 13*

I've learned that the secret of success in business is surprisingly simple: give people more than they expect and do it cheerfully.
— *Age 73*

I've learned that a good leader accepts bad news calmly.
— *Age 49*

I've learned that old women can get away with anything.
— *Age 40*

I've learned that what sounds like music to my teenagers sounds like a train wreck to me. — *Age 44*

I've learned that failures always blame someone else. — *Age 62*

I've learned that if I want the circumstances in my life to change for the better, I must change for the better. — *Age 42*

I've learned that when the light turns green, you had better look both ways before proceeding. — *Age 33*

I've learned that if you want to know who's the boss in a family, just check to see who holds the TV remote control.

—Age 48

I've learned that loneliness is not a way of life; it's a part of life.

—Age 33

I've learned that nothing very bad or very good ever lasts very long.

—Age 66

I've learned that the more a child feels valued, the better his values will be.

—Age 39

I've learned that sometimes I don't like to play
ball with Daddy because he gets mad when I
drop the ball.   *—Age 10*

I've learned that a loving, faithful wife is a man's
greatest treasure.   *—Age 68*

I've learned that the important thing is not what
others think of me, but what I think of me.   *—Age 38*

I've learned that no man is a match for a woman's
tears.   *—Age 49*

I've learned that a happy marriage multiplies joys and divides grief. — *Age 79*

I've learned that there is nothing more peaceful than a sleeping child. — *Age 30*

I've learned that you shouldn't discuss your success with people less successful than you. — *Age 50*

I've learned that when you've been angry at someone a long time, it's easier to stay mad than to make up. — *Age 24*

I've learned that women adapt to harsh conditions better and faster than men.
—Age 51

I've learned that a pat on the back and a sincere "You're doing a great job" can make someone's day.
—Age 49

I've learned that my worst decisions were made when I was angry.
—Age 62

I've learned that bigger is not always better, and that going faster is not necessarily progress.
—Age 73

I've learned that what some consider genius is often nothing more than good luck. —*Age 59*

■

I've learned that you can always get more money, but you can never get more time. —*Age 65*

■

I've learned that the song is right: love is lovelier the second time around. —*Age 34*

■

I've learned that when my wife and I finally get a night out without the kids, we spend most of the time talking about the kids. —*Age 29*

I've learned that when people aim for what they want out of life, most aim too low.

—Age 75

I've learned that an economist is the only person who can be right just 10 percent of the time and still get a paycheck.

—Age 62

I've learned that milk helps to keep your bones from bending over.

—Age 7

I've learned that meeting interesting people depends less on where you go than on who you are.

—Age 51

I've learned that it is very satisfying to work hard at work that's worth doing. — *Age 52*

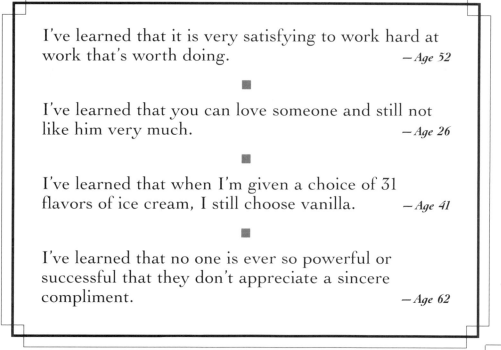

I've learned that you can love someone and still not like him very much. — *Age 26*

I've learned that when I'm given a choice of 31 flavors of ice cream, I still choose vanilla. — *Age 41*

I've learned that no one is ever so powerful or successful that they don't appreciate a sincere compliment. — *Age 62*

I've learned that the body has a miraculous capacity to heal itself. *—Age 78*

I've learned that if you talk to your friends more than to your wife about problems in your marriage, you're in serious trouble. *—Age 48*

I've learned that if you allow someone to make you angry, you have let him conquer you. *—Age 54*

I've learned that to trap mice, peanut butter works better than cheese. *—Age 36*

I've learned that people are more influenced by how much I care than by how much I know. *—Age 54*

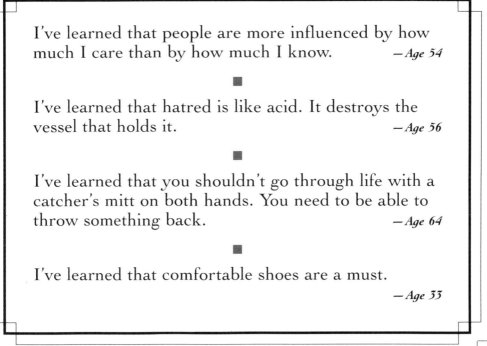

I've learned that hatred is like acid. It destroys the vessel that holds it. *—Age 56*

I've learned that you shouldn't go through life with a catcher's mitt on both hands. You need to be able to throw something back. *—Age 64*

I've learned that comfortable shoes are a must.

—Age 33

I've learned that marriages are meant to last a lifetime. When they don't, all the world suffers.

— Age 59

I've learned that the best way to attend to any problem is to hurry slowly.

— Age 68

I've learned that plotting revenge only allows the people who hurt you to hurt you longer.

— Age 40

I've learned that there are still some things I haven't made up my mind about yet.

— Age 91

I've learned that when I go to a cafeteria, I always eat too much. — *Age 38*

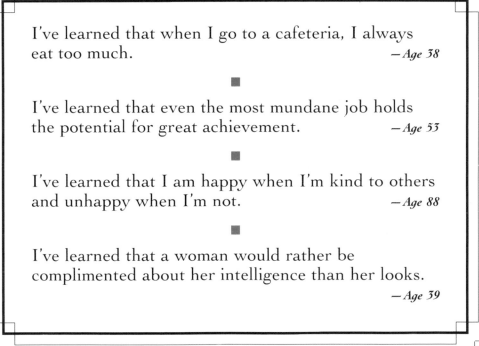

I've learned that even the most mundane job holds the potential for great achievement. — *Age 53*

I've learned that I am happy when I'm kind to others and unhappy when I'm not. — *Age 88*

I've learned that a woman would rather be complimented about her intelligence than her looks. — *Age 39*

I've learned that it's easy to go from the simple life to the fast track, but almost impossible to go back the other way. *— Age 44*

■

I've learned that my teacher always calls on me the one time I don't know the answer. *— Age 9*

■

I've learned that most people resist change, and yet it's the only thing that brings progress. *— Age 66*

■

I've learned that a new baby changes all your priorities. *— Age 28*

I've learned that regrets over yesterday and the fear of tomorrow are twin thieves that rob us of the moment. *—Age 29*

I've learned that enthusiasm and success just seem to go together. *—Age 44*

I've learned that you can never have too many smart people in your life. *—Age 48*

I've learned that life is like a blind date. Sometimes you just have to have a little faith. *—Age 23*

I've learned that you form a committee to "study the matter" when you really don't want to do anything.

—Age 43

■

I've learned that you never get rewarded for the things you intended to do.

—Age 76

■

I've learned how to hold animals without killing them.

—Age 5

■

I've learned that you shouldn't expect life's very best if you're not giving it your very best.

—Age 51

I've learned that my best friend is my teddy bear. He never tells my secrets.   *— Age 17*

■

I've learned that the only time I want to sleep late is when I can't.   *— Age 29*

■

I've learned not to waste time worrying about the things I can't change.   *— Age 72*

■

I've learned that a marriage can survive almost anything except the husband staying home all day.

— Age 58

I've learned that the trick is to live a long time without growing old. —*Age 73*

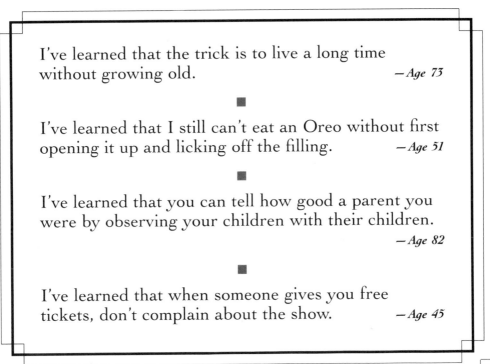

I've learned that I still can't eat an Oreo without first opening it up and licking off the filling. —*Age 51*

I've learned that you can tell how good a parent you were by observing your children with their children. —*Age 82*

I've learned that when someone gives you free tickets, don't complain about the show. —*Age 45*

I've learned that the higher up you go in a corporation, the nicer the people are and the better manners they have.
—Age 55

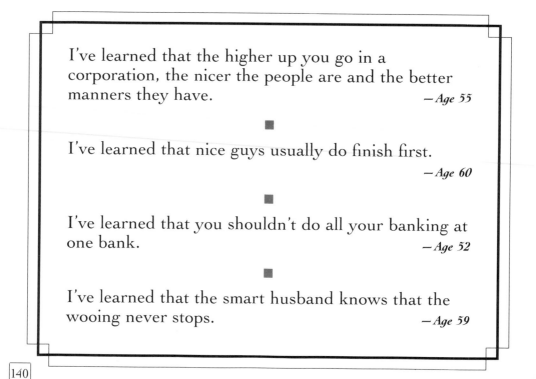

I've learned that nice guys usually do finish first.
—Age 60

I've learned that you shouldn't do all your banking at one bank.
—Age 52

I've learned that the smart husband knows that the wooing never stops.
—Age 59

I've learned that kids need hugs more than they need things. *— Age 43*

I've learned that everybody likes to be asked his or her opinion. *— Age 71*

I've learned that the trip is often more fun than the destination. *— Age 62*

I've learned that if your teenager doesn't think you're a real embarrassment and a hard-nosed bore, you're probably not doing your job. *— Age 44*

I've learned that it's not enough to have a wonderful life. You must recognize the fact and be grateful for it.

—Age 74

■

I've learned that talking about your problems doesn't always help.

—Age 15

■

I've learned that you should never play for a tie score. Go for the win.

—Age 41

■

I've learned that position can be bought, but respect must be earned.

—Age 51

I've learned that the people who say, "Money isn't everything," usually have plenty of it. —*Age 66*

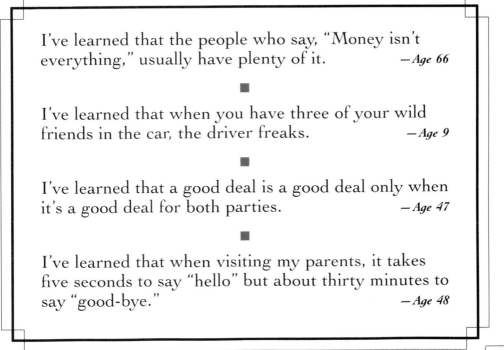

I've learned that when you have three of your wild friends in the car, the driver freaks. —*Age 9*

I've learned that a good deal is a good deal only when it's a good deal for both parties. —*Age 47*

I've learned that when visiting my parents, it takes five seconds to say "hello" but about thirty minutes to say "good-bye." —*Age 48*

I've learned that fame is written in ice and eventually
the sun comes out.
— Age 57

I've learned that I am my child's most important
teacher.
— Age 32

I've learned that I don't understand women and I
never will.
— Age 84

I've learned that kind words and good deeds are
eternal. You never know where their influence
will end.
— Age 51

I've learned that if you ask someone, "I wonder if you could please help me?" you will almost always get a positive response. *—Age 57*

■

I've learned that you shouldn't buy cheap shoes, cheap tools, or cheap toilet paper. *—Age 33*

■

I've learned that my most important piece of office equipment is a wastebasket. *—Age 54*

■

I've learned that people who lie *for* you will lie *to* you. *—Age 43*

I've learned that the best tranquilizer is a clear conscience.

—Age 76

I've learned to be generous with praise but cautious with promises.

—Age 54

I've learned that the faults I have now are exactly the ones my parents tried to correct when I was a child.

—Age 40

I've learned that to get the right answer, you have to ask the right question.

—Age 39

I've learned that many people give up just when they are about to achieve success. — *Age 48*

I've learned that it's never too late to improve yourself. — *Age 85*

I've learned that relationships are more important than rules. — *Age 51*

I've learned that it has taken me sixty-one years to learn to do what my granddaughter calls "mellowing out." — *Age 66*

I've learned that it takes as much time and energy to wish as it does to plan.
—Age 49

I've learned that there's never a snow day on the day I have a big test.
—Age 12

I've learned that we grow only when we push ourselves beyond what we already know.
—Age 53

I've learned that a time comes when you would give all you possess to have your grown children young again, if only for one day.
—Age 60

I've learned that sometimes life hands you situations when all you can do is put one foot in front of the other and live moment to moment. — *Age 66*

I've learned that it makes me happy to see my parents holding hands. — *Age 13*

I've learned that people who have mastered the art of living seem to be guided by an internal compass. They might not always stay on track, but they have a way of always returning to the proper course. — *Age 63*

I've learned that you can never have too many
friends. *—Age 16*

I've learned that if you don't feel like being pleasant,
courteous, and kind, act that way and the feelings
will come. *—Age 38*

I've learned that there are people who love you
dearly but just don't know how to show it. *—Age 41*

I've learned that when things get easy, it's easy to
stop growing. *—Age 53*

I've learned that when you have a wonderful wife, tell others — but be sure to tell her too.

—Age 51

I've learned that you should say your prayers every night.

—Age 9

I've learned that people are in such a hurry to get to the "good life" that they often rush right past it.

—Age 72

I've learned that you shouldn't speak unless you can improve on the silence.

—Age 62

I've learned that history is not what actually happened, but what people reported to have happened. — *Age 60*

I've learned that people can change, so give them the benefit of the doubt. — *Age 14*

I've learned that phone calls after midnight seldom bring good news. — *Age 63*

I've learned that if you wish to do business with honest people, you must be an honest person. — *Age 55*

I've learned that I am slightly suspicious of people who fill their offices with awards and pictures of their family.

—Age 65

I've learned that you often take out your frustrations on the people you love the most.

—Age 29

I've learned that you can inherit wealth but never wisdom.

—Age 51

I've learned that the older I get, the less attention I get.

—Age 6

I've learned that it's never too late to heal an injured relationship.

—Age 57

I've learned that the little sayings you learn as a child, such as the Golden Rule, are actually important.

—Age 15

I've learned never to underestimate the potential and power of the human spirit.

—Age 82

I've learned that you have little chance of finding the caring, supportive husband of your dreams in a bar.

—Age 29

I've learned that for a happy day, look for something bright and beautiful in nature. Listen for a beautiful sound, speak a kind word to some person, and do something nice for someone without their knowledge.

—Age 85

I've learned that there is always someone who cares.

—Age 75

I've learned that about 90 percent of the things that happen to me are good and only about 10 percent are bad. To be happy, I just have to focus on the 90 percent.

—Age 54

I've learned that it's not what happens to people that's important. It's what they do about it. —*Age 10*

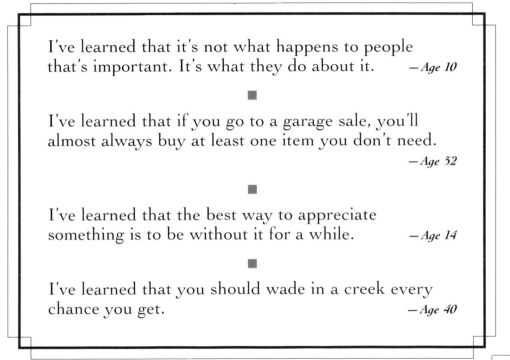

I've learned that if you go to a garage sale, you'll almost always buy at least one item you don't need.
—*Age 52*

I've learned that the best way to appreciate something is to be without it for a while. —*Age 14*

I've learned that you should wade in a creek every chance you get. —*Age 40*

I've learned that no matter how bad it gets, when my child hugs my neck and kisses me and says, "Don't worry, everything will be OK," I know I'll be able to make it.
—Age 28

I've learned that you don't miss fighting with your sister until she's left for college.
—Age 14

I've learned that every day you should reach out and touch someone. People love that human touch — holding hands, a warm hug, or just a friendly pat on the back.
—Age 85

I've learned to keep looking ahead. There are still so many good books to read, sunsets to see, friends to visit, and old dogs to take walks with. —*Age 86*

I've learned that you shouldn't do anything that wouldn't make your mother proud. —*Age 51*

I've learned that I still have a lot to learn. —*Age 92*

Dear Reader,

If life has taught you a thing or two and you would like to pass it on, please write it down with your name, age, and address and mail it to me. I would welcome the opportunity of sharing it with other readers in a future book. Thanks!

H. Jackson Brown, Jr.
P. O. Box 150014
Nashville, TN 37215